Foreword

When it comes to the world of culinary delights, few experiences are
as the realm of mezes, the art of small plates and appetizers. In th
on a delectable journey, exploring the rich tapestry of flavors, tra
that come together on the small plates of the Mediterranean and beyond.

Mezes, or as they're known in various parts of the world—tapas, antipasti, hors d'oeuvres, or
simply appetizers—represent the heart and soul of social dining. These miniature masterpieces
have the power to transport us to far-off lands, evoke cherished memories, and bring loved
ones closer around the table. The act of sharing mezes is a celebration of life, an
expression of hospitality, and a reminder that the joy of eating goes far beyond sustenance.

As you delve into the recipes and stories contained within these pages, you'll discover a
world of culinary ingenuity. From the silky smoothness of hummus to the vibrant flavors of
tabouleh, from the comforting familiarity of bruschetta to the boldness of marinated
artichoke hearts, the meze world is a kaleidoscope of tastes and textures.

But this book is more than just a collection of recipes; it's a tribute to the cultures and
histories that have contributed to this rich tapestry of flavors. It's an invitation to savor
the moments when we gather around the table, break bread, and share not just food, but our
stories, laughter, and love.

Whether you're a seasoned home cook or a culinary explorer just beginning your journey, the
recipes and insights within these pages will inspire you to create your own meze magic.
You'll learn the art of balancing bold and subtle flavors, discover the joy of mixing and
matching, and master the art of the perfect pairing. With every recipe, you'll uncover the
secrets of crafting the perfect bite, one that will leave a lasting impression on your guests
and create memories that linger long after the last dish is cleared.

So, open this book, turn the page, and let the adventure begin. Explore the world of mezes
with an open heart and an eager palate. Prepare to be transported to bustling Mediterranean
markets, to cozy Mediterranean taverns, and to the warm kitchens of passionate cooks who've
perfected these small wonders over generations.

Whether you're planning an elegant soirée, a casual gathering of friends, or simply a cozy
evening for yourself, these mezes will inspire you to make every meal an occasion to
remember. From the familiar to the exotic, the comforting to the surprising, these mezes are
an invitation to celebrate the beauty of the small plate and the joy of shared culinary
adventures.

As you embark on this flavorful journey, may your kitchen be filled with the delightful
aromas of fresh herbs, spices, and the promise of memorable meals. May your table be
surrounded by friends and loved ones, and may your heart be warmed by the simple act of
sharing good food and good company.

With this book in your hands, I invite you to immerse yourself in the world of mezes and
embrace the power of small plates to create big impressions.

Bon appétit!   Alvi Kaston

Humus

Ingredients:

- 1 can (15 ounces) of chickpeas (garbanzo beans), drained and rinsed
- 1/4 cup fresh lemon juice (about 1 large lemon)
- 1/4 cup well-stirred tahini (sesame paste)
- 1 small garlic clove, minced
- 2 tablespoons extra-virgin olive oil, plus more for serving
- 1/2 teaspoon ground cumin
- Salt, to taste
- 2 to 3 tablespoons water
- 1/2 teaspoon paprika, for garnish (optional)
- Chopped fresh parsley, for garnish (optional)

Instructions:

Combine Ingredients: In a food processor, combine the chickpeas, lemon juice, tahini, minced garlic, olive oil, cumin, and a pinch of salt. Process until smooth.

Blend and Adjust Consistency: While the food processor is running, slowly add 2 to 3 tablespoons of water to thin the hummus and achieve your desired consistency. You can add more water if needed.

Taste and Adjust: Taste the hummus and add more salt or lemon juice if desired. Adjust the flavors to your liking.

Serve: Transfer the hummus to a serving bowl. Drizzle some olive oil on top and sprinkle with paprika and chopped fresh parsley for garnish if you like.

Enjoy: Serve your homemade hummus with pita bread, fresh vegetables, or as a dip for your favorite snacks. It's also great as a spread in sandwiches or wraps.

Storage: Store any leftover hummus in an airtight container in the refrigerator for up to a week. Drizzle a little extra olive oil on top to help keep it fresh.

Tzatziki

Ingredients:

- 1 cucumber, finely grated
- 1 1/2 cups Greek yogurt (full-fat or low-fat)
- 2-3 cloves garlic, minced
- 1-2 tablespoons fresh lemon juice (to taste)
- 2 tablespoons extra-virgin olive oil
- 1 tablespoon fresh dill, finely chopped (or 1 teaspoon dried dill)
- 1 tablespoon fresh mint, finely chopped (optional)
- Salt and black pepper, to taste

Instructions:

1. **Prepare the Cucumber:** Start by grating the cucumber using a fine grater. Place the grated cucumber in a clean kitchen towel or cheesecloth and squeeze out as much liquid as possible. You want the cucumber to be as dry as you can get it.
2. **Combine Ingredients:** In a mixing bowl, combine the grated and drained cucumber, Greek yogurt, minced garlic, lemon juice, olive oil, chopped dill, and mint (if using). Mix everything together until well combined.
3. **Season:** Season the tzatziki with salt and black pepper to taste. Start with a pinch of salt and adjust according to your preference.
4. **Chill:** Cover the tzatziki and refrigerate for at least an hour before serving. This allows the flavors to meld together.
5. **Serve:** Serve tzatziki as a dip with pita bread, fresh vegetables, or as a sauce for gyros, souvlaki, or grilled meats.
6. **Optional Garnish:** You can drizzle a bit of extra olive oil and sprinkle some fresh dill on top for garnish if desired.
7. **Storage:** Tzatziki can be stored in an airtight container in the refrigerator for a few days. It may thicken over time, so you can stir in a little extra yogurt or a splash of water to reach your desired consistency before serving.

Baba Ghanoush

Ingredients:

- 2 medium-sized eggplants
- 1/4 cup tahini (sesame paste)
- 2-3 cloves garlic, minced
- 2 tablespoons lemon juice (or more to taste)
- 2 tablespoons extra-virgin olive oil, plus more for drizzling
- 1/2 teaspoon ground cumin
- Salt and black pepper, to taste
- Chopped fresh parsley, for garnish (optional)

Instructions:

1. **Roast the Eggplants:** Preheat your oven to 400°F (200°C). Pierce the eggplants several times with a fork to allow steam to escape during roasting. Place them on a baking sheet and roast in the preheated oven for about 45-60 minutes, or until the eggplants are tender and the skin is charred. You can also roast them on a grill for a smoky flavor.

2. **Cool and Peel:** Remove the roasted eggplants from the oven and let them cool for a bit. Once they are cool enough to handle, peel off the charred skin. You should be left with the soft flesh.

3. **Blend the Ingredients:** In a food processor, combine the roasted eggplant flesh, tahini, minced garlic, lemon juice, olive oil, ground cumin, and a pinch of salt and black pepper. Process until the mixture is smooth and creamy. Taste and adjust the seasoning by adding more lemon juice, salt, or pepper as needed.

4. **Chill and Serve:** Transfer the baba ghanoush to a serving bowl. Drizzle with a bit of olive oil and garnish with chopped fresh parsley if desired. Refrigerate for at least an hour before serving to allow the flavors to meld together.

5. **Enjoy:** Serve baba ghanoush with pita bread, crackers, or fresh vegetable sticks for dipping.

6. **Storage:** It can be stored in an airtight container in the refrigerator for a few days. It's normal for it to thicken a bit in the fridge, so you can stir in a little extra olive oil before serving if needed.

Tabouleh

Ingredients:
For the Salad:
- 1 cup fine bulgur wheat
- 1 1/2 cups boiling water
- 2 cups finely chopped fresh parsley (about 2 large bunches)
- 1/2 cup finely chopped fresh mint leaves
- 2 medium tomatoes, diced
- 1 cucumber, diced
- 1/2 cup finely chopped green onions (white and green parts)
- Salt and black pepper, to taste

For the Dressing:
- 1/4 cup extra-virgin olive oil
- 1/4 cup fresh lemon juice (about 2 lemons)
- 1-2 cloves garlic, minced
- 1/2 teaspoon ground cumin (optional)

Instructions:
1. **Prepare the Bulgur Wheat:** Place the bulgur wheat in a heatproof bowl. Pour the boiling water over it, cover with a lid or plastic wrap, and let it sit for about 20-30 minutes, or until the bulgur is tender and has absorbed the water. Fluff the bulgur with a fork.
2. **Chop the Herbs and Vegetables:** While the bulgur is soaking, chop the fresh parsley, mint leaves, tomatoes, cucumber, and green onions finely. You want everything to be finely chopped for a good texture.
3. **Prepare the Dressing:** In a small bowl, whisk together the olive oil, lemon juice, minced garlic, and ground cumin (if using). Taste and adjust the seasoning by adding more lemon juice, garlic, or cumin as needed.
4. **Combine and Mix:** In a large mixing bowl, combine the soaked and fluffed bulgur with the chopped herbs, tomatoes, cucumber, and green onions. Mix everything together.
5. **Dress the Salad:** Pour the dressing over the salad and toss well to coat all the ingredients. Season with salt and black pepper to taste.
6. **Chill and Serve:** Refrigerate the tabouleh for at least an hour before serving to allow the flavors to meld together. It's even better if you let it chill for a few hours.
7. **Enjoy:** Serve tabouleh as a refreshing side dish or as a light and healthy main course. It's often served with pita bread or as a topping for grilled meats.

Falafel

Ingredients:

For the Falafel:

- 1 1/2 cups dried chickpeas (or use canned chickpeas, drained)
- 1 small onion, roughly chopped
- 1/4 cup fresh parsley, chopped
- 1/4 cup fresh cilantro, chopped
- 3-4 cloves garlic
- 1 1/2 tablespoons ground cumin
- 1 1/2 teaspoons ground coriander
- 1/4 teaspoon cayenne pepper (optional, for heat)
- Salt and black pepper, to taste
- 1 teaspoon baking powder
- 4-6 tablespoons all-purpose flour
- Vegetable oil, for frying

Instructions:

1. **Prepare the Chickpeas:** If using dried chickpeas, rinse and soak them in cold water for at least 12 hours or overnight. Drain well. If using canned chickpeas, rinse and drain them thoroughly.
2. **Combine Ingredients:** In a food processor, combine the chickpeas, chopped onion, parsley, cilantro, garlic, cumin, coriander, cayenne pepper (if using), salt, and black pepper. Pulse the mixture until it becomes a coarse paste but not a smooth puree. You want some texture.
3. **Add Baking Powder and Flour:** Sprinkle the baking powder and 4 tablespoons of flour over the mixture. Pulse again to combine. The mixture should hold together when pressed into a ball. If it's too wet, add more flour, one tablespoon at a time, and pulse until the right consistency is achieved.
4. **Chill the Mixture:** Transfer the falafel mixture to a bowl, cover it, and refrigerate for at least 1 hour. Chilling helps the mixture firm up and makes it easier to shape into patties.
5. **Shape the Falafel:** Take small portions of the mixture and shape them into small patties, about 1 1/2 inches (4 cm) in diameter. You can make them round or slightly flattened.
6. **Fry the Falafel:** Heat about 2 inches (5 cm) of vegetable oil in a deep skillet or frying pan over medium-high heat. When the oil is hot (about 350°F or 175°C), carefully add the falafel patties a few at a time. Fry until they are deep golden brown and crispy, about 3-4 minutes per side. Use a slotted spoon to remove them from the oil and place them on paper towels to drain excess oil.
7. **Serve:** Serve the falafel in pita bread or flatbreads with sliced vegetables and your choice of sauce (tahini or yogurt sauce). You can also add pickles or olives for extra flavor.

Dolmas

For the Dolma Filling:

- 1 cup long-grain white rice
- 1 small onion, finely chopped
- 2 cloves garlic, minced
- 2 tablespoons extra-virgin olive oil
- 1/2 cup fresh parsley, finely chopped
- 1/4 cup fresh dill, finely chopped
- 1/4 cup fresh mint, finely chopped
- 1/4 cup pine nuts (optional)
- 1/4 cup currants or raisins (optional)
- Salt and black pepper, to taste
- 1 teaspoon ground cumin
- 1 teaspoon ground coriander
- Juice of 1 lemon

For the Grape Leaves and Assembly:

- 1 jar of grape leaves in brine, drained and rinsed (about 50 leaves)
- 2-3 tablespoons extra-virgin olive oil
- Juice of 1-2 lemons
- Water, as needed
- Lemon slices and fresh herbs for garnish (optional)

Instructions:

1. **Prepare the Grape Leaves:** Carefully remove the grape leaves from the jar, unfold them, and rinse them under cold water to remove excess brine. Place them in a colander to drain.
2. **Prepare the Filling:** In a large skillet, heat the olive oil over medium heat. Add the chopped onions and garlic and sauté for about 2-3 minutes until they soften. Stir in the rice and continue to cook, stirring frequently, for another 3-4 minutes until the rice is lightly toasted.
3. **Add Herbs and Spices:** Stir in the chopped parsley, dill, mint, pine nuts (if using), currants or raisins (if using), salt, black pepper, ground cumin, and ground coriander. Cook for an additional 2 minutes to let the flavors meld together. Remove the mixture from the heat and stir in the lemon juice.
4. **Prepare the Grape Leaves for Stuffing:** To make it easier to roll the dolmas, you may want to trim the stems off the grape leaves and remove any tough veins.
5. **Roll the Dolmas:** Place a grape leaf, shiny side down, on a clean surface. Add about a tablespoon of the rice mixture near the stem end of the leaf. Fold in the sides and roll it up tightly into a cigar-shaped roll. Repeat with the remaining grape leaves and filling.
6. **Layer and Cook the Dolmas:** In a large pot, arrange a layer of grape leaves on the bottom to prevent sticking. Place the rolled dolmas, seam side down, in the pot, packing them closely together in layers. Drizzle the olive oil and lemon juice over the top layer. Place a heavy plate or a lid on top of the dolmas to keep them in place during cooking.
7. **Cook the Dolmas:** Add enough water to the pot to cover the dolmas. Cover the pot and cook over low heat for about 40-45 minutes, or until the rice is cooked

Spanakopita

Ingredients:

For the Filling:

- 1 pound (450g) fresh spinach, washed, trimmed, and coarsely chopped
- 1 cup crumbled feta cheese
- 1/2 cup ricotta cheese or cottage cheese (optional, for creaminess)
- 1/2 cup grated Parmesan cheese
- 1 small onion, finely chopped
- 2-3 cloves garlic, minced
- 2 tablespoons olive oil
- 1/4 cup fresh dill, finely chopped
- Salt and black pepper, to taste
- Pinch of ground nutmeg (optional)

For the Phyllo Layers:

- 1 package (16 ounces) phyllo dough, thawed according to package instructions
- 1/2 cup (1 stick) unsalted butter, melted
- Olive oil or cooking spray for greasing the baking dish

Instructions:

1. **Prepare the Filling:** In a large skillet, heat the olive oil over medium heat. Add the chopped onions and garlic and sauté until they become translucent, about 2-3 minutes.
2. **Add Spinach:** Add the chopped spinach to the skillet in batches, allowing it to wilt down as you go. Sauté the spinach until it's completely wilted and any excess moisture has evaporated. This should take about 5-7 minutes. Remove the skillet from the heat and let the spinach cool.
3. **Drain and Squeeze:** Once the spinach has cooled, use your hands to squeeze out any excess moisture. You want the spinach to be as dry as possible.
4. **Prepare the Filling Mixture:** In a large bowl, combine the squeezed spinach, crumbled feta cheese, ricotta or cottage cheese (if using), grated Parmesan cheese, chopped dill, salt, black pepper, and a pinch of ground nutmeg (if using). Mix everything together until well combined. Taste and adjust the seasoning if needed.
5. **Preheat the Oven:** Preheat your oven to 375°F (190°C). Grease a 9x13-inch baking dish with olive oil or cooking spray.
6. **Assemble the Spanakopita:** Carefully unroll the phyllo dough sheets on a clean, dry surface. Keep them covered with a damp kitchen towel to prevent them from drying out.
7. **Layer the Phyllo Sheets:** Place one sheet of phyllo dough in the greased baking dish, allowing the excess to hang over the sides. Brush it generously with melted butter. Repeat this process, layering and buttering each sheet, until you have about 8-10 sheets layered in the bottom of the dish.
8. **Add the Filling:** Spread the spinach and cheese mixture evenly over the phyllo dough layers.
9. **Finish with More Phyllo:** Continue layering the remaining phyllo sheets, brushing each one with melted butter, until you've used them all. Make sure to brush the top sheet generously with butter as well.
10. **Bake:** Using a sharp knife, score the top layer of phyllo into squares or diamonds. This will make it easier to cut after baking. Bake in the preheated oven for about 45-50 minutes, or until the spanakopita is golden brown and crisp.
11. **Cool and Serve:** Allow the spanakopita to cool for a few minutes before cutting and serving. It can be served warm or at room temperature.

Muhammara

Ingredients:

- 3 red bell peppers
- 1 cup walnuts, toasted
- 1/2 cup breadcrumbs (you can use fresh breadcrumbs or toasted bread)
- 2-3 cloves garlic, minced
- 2 tablespoons pomegranate molasses
- 2 tablespoons lemon juice (about 1 lemon)
- 1 teaspoon ground cumin
- 1 teaspoon ground coriander
- 1/2 teaspoon red pepper flakes (adjust to taste)
- Salt, to taste
- 1/4 cup extra-virgin olive oil, plus more for drizzling
- Fresh parsley, chopped, for garnish (optional)
- Pomegranate seeds, for garnish (optional)

Instructions:

1. **Roast the Red Peppers:** Preheat your oven to 450°F (230°C). Place the red bell peppers on a baking sheet lined with aluminum foil. Roast the peppers in the preheated oven for 25-30 minutes, or until the skin is charred and blistered, turning them occasionally to ensure even roasting. Remove the peppers from the oven and immediately transfer them to a bowl. Cover the bowl with plastic wrap and let the peppers steam for about 15 minutes. This will make it easier to peel off the skin.
2. **Peel and Seed the Peppers:** After steaming, peel the charred skin off the roasted peppers and remove the seeds and membranes. Cut the peppers into smaller pieces.
3. **Toast the Walnuts:** While the peppers are steaming, toast the walnuts in a dry skillet over medium heat for about 3-5 minutes until fragrant. Be careful not to burn them. Remove from heat and let them cool.
4. **Blend the Ingredients:** In a food processor, combine the roasted red peppers, toasted walnuts, breadcrumbs, minced garlic, pomegranate molasses, lemon juice, ground cumin, ground coriander, red pepper flakes, and salt. Pulse until the mixture is well blended and forms a thick, slightly coarse paste.
5. **Add Olive Oil:** With the food processor running, gradually add the olive oil in a steady stream until the muhammara becomes smooth and well combined. You may need to scrape down the sides of the food processor bowl and blend again.
6. **Adjust Seasoning:** Taste the muhammara and adjust the seasoning as needed. You can add more salt, lemon juice, or red pepper flakes to suit your taste.
7. **Chill and Serve:** Transfer the muhammara to a serving bowl. Drizzle with a bit of extra olive oil and garnish with chopped fresh parsley and pomegranate seeds if desired. Refrigerate for at least 1 hour before serving to allow the flavors to meld together.
8. **Enjoy:** Serve muhammara as a dip with pita bread, fresh vegetables, or as a condiment for grilled meats or sandwiches.

Feta Cheese and Olives

Ingredients:

- 8 ounces (about 1 cup) feta cheese, block or crumbled
- 1 cup mixed olives (such as Kalamata, green, or black olives)
- 2-3 tablespoons extra-virgin olive oil
- 1-2 cloves garlic, minced (optional)
- 1 teaspoon dried oregano (or fresh oregano leaves for garnish)
- Freshly ground black pepper, to taste
- Red pepper flakes (optional, for added heat)
- Lemon zest (optional, for extra flavor)
- Fresh parsley or basil leaves for garnish (optional)
- Sliced baguette, pita bread, or crackers for serving

1. **Prepare the Feta Cheese:**
   - If you have a block of feta cheese, you can cut it into smaller cubes or slices. Alternatively, if you have crumbled feta, you can use it as is.
2. **Marinate the Olives:**
   - In a small bowl, combine the mixed olives with 2-3 tablespoons of extra-virgin olive oil. If desired, add minced garlic for extra flavor and a pinch of red pepper flakes for some heat. Toss the olives to coat them evenly in the oil and seasonings.
3. **Assemble the Dish:**
   - Arrange the feta cheese and marinated olives on a serving platter or plate. You can place the feta cheese in the center and surround it with the olives, or you can mix them together.
4. **Season and Garnish:**
   - Sprinkle the dried oregano over the feta cheese and olives. You can also add freshly ground black pepper for extra flavor. If desired, grate some lemon zest over the top for a burst of citrus flavor.
5. **Garnish and Serve:**
   - For a fresh touch, garnish the dish with fresh parsley or basil leaves. These herbs add color and flavor to the appetizer.
6. **Serve with Bread or Crackers:**
   - Serve the feta cheese and olives with slices of baguette, pita bread, or your favorite crackers. The bread or crackers can be used to scoop up the cheese and olives.
7. **Enjoy:**
   - This simple feta cheese and olives appetizer is ready to enjoy. It's perfect for a party, as a starter for a Mediterranean-themed meal, or as a quick snack.

Labneh

Ingredients:

- 2 cups of full-fat plain yogurt (Greek yogurt works well)
- 1/2 teaspoon salt (adjust to taste)
- Olive oil (for drizzling, optional)
- Fresh herbs, such as mint or parsley, for garnish (optional)

Instructions:

1. **Prepare the Cucumber:** After peeling and seeding the cucumber, grate it using a fine grater. Place the grated cucumber in a clean kitchen towel or cheesecloth and squeeze out as much liquid as possible. You want the cucumber to be as dry as you can get it.
2. **Mix the Yogurt:** In a mixing bowl, combine the plain Greek yogurt and minced garlic. Mix well until the yogurt and garlic are thoroughly combined.
3. **Add Cucumber and Herbs:** Add the grated and squeezed cucumber, chopped fresh mint, and fresh dill to the yogurt mixture. Mix everything together until well combined.
4. **Season and Add Lemon Juice:** Season the cacık with salt and black pepper to taste. Add the fresh lemon juice and extra-virgin olive oil. Mix again to incorporate all the ingredients.
5. **Chill:** Cover the cacık and refrigerate for at least an hour before serving. This allows the flavors to meld together.
6. **Serve:** Serve cacık chilled, garnished with a sprig of fresh mint leaves if desired. You can also add a few ice cubes to keep it extra cold, especially on a hot day.
7. **Enjoy:** Cacık is great as a side dish, dip for pita bread or vegetables, or as a refreshing accompaniment to grilled meats.
8. **Storage:** Leftover cacık can be stored in an airtight container in the refrigerator for a day or two. Stir it before serving to recombine any separated liquids.

Cacık

Ingredients:

- 2 cups plain Greek yogurt
- 1 cucumber, peeled, seeded, and grated
- 2-3 cloves garlic, minced
- 2 tablespoons fresh mint, finely chopped (or 1-2 teaspoons dried mint)
- 1-2 tablespoons fresh dill, finely chopped
- 1 tablespoon extra-virgin olive oil
- 1 tablespoon fresh lemon juice (about 1/2 lemon)
- Salt and black pepper, to taste
- Ice cubes (optional, for serving)
- Fresh mint leaves for garnish (optional)

Instructions:

1. **Strain the Yogurt:**
   - Place a clean piece of cheesecloth, a nut milk bag, or a clean kitchen towel in a fine-mesh strainer or sieve. Set the strainer over a deep bowl.
2. **Mix with Salt:**
   - In a separate bowl, mix the plain yogurt and salt together until well combined. The salt helps to enhance the flavor and aids in the thickening process.
3. **Transfer to the Strainer:**
   - Pour the yogurt mixture into the prepared strainer. Gather the corners of the cheesecloth or towel and tie them together to form a bundle.
4. **Hang and Drain:**
   - Hang the bundle over the strainer so that it's suspended over the bowl. Allow the liquid (whey) to drain from the yogurt into the bowl beneath. You can hang it from a cupboard handle or place it in the refrigerator.
5. **Drain to Desired Consistency:**
   - Let the yogurt strain for at least 12 hours, but you can leave it longer for a thicker labneh. The longer you drain it, the thicker and creamier it will become. Overnight is a common duration.
6. **Unwrap and Serve:**
   - Carefully unwrap the labneh from the cheesecloth or towel and transfer it to a serving dish. The consistency should be similar to cream cheese, but you can make it thicker or creamier depending on your preference.
7. **Garnish and Serve:**
   - Drizzle with olive oil and garnish with fresh herbs, if desired. Serve your homemade labneh with pita bread, fresh vegetables, or as a spread on toast or crackers.
8. **Storage:**
   - Store any leftover labneh in an airtight container in the refrigerator. It will keep for about 1-2 weeks.

Kısır

Ingredients:

For the Salad:

- 1 cup fine bulgur wheat
- 1 1/2 cups boiling water
- 1 cup finely chopped fresh parsley
- 1/2 cup finely chopped fresh mint
- 2-3 green onions, finely chopped
- 1 small cucumber, finely diced
- 2 medium tomatoes, finely diced
- 1/2 red bell pepper, finely diced
- 1/2 yellow bell pepper, finely diced (optional)
- 1/4 cup black olives, pitted and chopped (optional)
- 1/4 cup chopped walnuts (optional)
- Salt and black pepper, to taste
- Lettuce leaves, for serving (optional)

For the Dressing:

- 3-4 tablespoons extra-virgin olive oil
- 3 tablespoons pomegranate molasses
- Juice of 2 lemons
- 2-3 cloves garlic, minced
- 1-2 teaspoons ground cumin
- 1-2 teaspoons ground red pepper or paprika (adjust to taste)
- Salt and black pepper, to taste

Instructions:

1. **Prepare the Bulgur Wheat:** Place the bulgur wheat in a heatproof bowl. Pour the boiling water over it, cover with a lid or plastic wrap, and let it sit for about 20-30 minutes, or until the bulgur is tender and has absorbed the water. Fluff the bulgur with a fork.
2. **Chop the Vegetables and Herbs:** While the bulgur is soaking, finely chop the fresh parsley, fresh mint, green onions, cucumber, tomatoes, and bell peppers. If you're using black olives and walnuts, chop them as well.
3. **Prepare the Dressing:** In a separate bowl, whisk together the extra-virgin olive oil, pomegranate molasses, lemon juice, minced garlic, ground cumin, ground red pepper or paprika, salt, and black pepper. Taste and adjust the seasoning by adding more lemon juice, pomegranate molasses, or spices as needed.
4. **Combine and Mix:** In a large mixing bowl, combine the soaked and fluffed bulgur with the chopped vegetables, herbs, and optional olives and walnuts. Mix everything together.
5. **Dress the Salad:** Pour the dressing over the salad and toss well to coat all the ingredients. Make sure the dressing is evenly distributed.
6. **Chill and Serve:** Cover the kısır and refrigerate for at least 1 hour before serving to allow the flavors to meld together.
7. **Serve:** Kısır can be served on a bed of lettuce leaves or on its own as an appetizer or side dish. It's commonly wrapped in lettuce leaves and eaten by hand.

Saganaki

Ingredients:

- 8 ounces (about 1 cup) kefalotyri cheese (substitute with graviera or halloumi if unavailable)
- 1/4 cup all-purpose flour, for dredging
- 2-3 tablespoons olive oil, for frying
- 1-2 cloves garlic, minced (optional, for added flavor)
- 1-2 tablespoons ouzo or brandy (optional, for flambéing)
- Juice of 1 lemon
- Freshly ground black pepper, to taste
- Chopped fresh parsley, for garnish
- Crusty bread or pita, for serving

Instructions:

1. **Slice the Cheese:** Cut the kefalotyri cheese into thick slices or wedges. If you're using halloumi, slice it similarly.
2. **Dredge in Flour:** Dredge the cheese slices in all-purpose flour, making sure they are evenly coated. Shake off any excess flour.
3. **Heat the Olive Oil:** In a large skillet, heat 2-3 tablespoons of olive oil over medium-high heat. If using minced garlic, add it to the hot oil and sauté briefly until fragrant, about 30 seconds.
4. **Fry the Cheese:** Carefully place the flour-coated cheese slices in the hot oil. Fry them for about 2-3 minutes on each side, or until they are golden brown and crispy. Be gentle when flipping the cheese to avoid breaking it.
5. **Flambé (Optional):** If you'd like to flambé the saganaki for added drama and flavor, remove the skillet from the heat, add 1-2 tablespoons of ouzo or brandy to the pan, and carefully ignite it with a long lighter or match. Allow the flames to subside naturally.
6. **Add Lemon Juice:** Squeeze the juice of one lemon over the fried cheese slices. The lemon juice will create a delightful sizzling and bubbling effect.
7. **Season:** Season the saganaki with freshly ground black pepper to taste.
8. **Garnish:** Sprinkle chopped fresh parsley over the top of the saganaki for a burst of freshness.
9. **Serve:** Transfer the saganaki to a serving plate and serve immediately while it's hot. You can enjoy it with slices of crusty bread or warm pita bread for dipping.
10. **Enjoy:** Saganaki is best enjoyed right away while the cheese is still warm and gooey. It's a delightful appetizer or meze dish.

Skordalia

Ingredients:

- 4-5 large russet potatoes, peeled and cut into chunks
- 6-8 cloves of garlic, minced
- 1/2 cup extra-virgin olive oil, plus extra for drizzling
- 2-3 tablespoons white wine vinegar or fresh lemon juice (adjust to taste)
- Salt, to taste
- Freshly ground black pepper, to taste
- Chopped fresh parsley, for garnish (optional)
- Kalamata olives, for garnish (optional)
- Sliced cucumbers and warm pita bread, for serving

Instructions:

1. **Boil the Potatoes:** Place the potato chunks in a large pot of salted boiling water. Cook them until they are fork-tender, usually about 15-20 minutes. Drain the potatoes and let them cool slightly.
2. **Mash the Potatoes:** While the potatoes are still warm, mash them with a potato masher or fork until they are smooth and creamy. You can also use a ricer for an even smoother texture.
3. **Prepare the Garlic Paste:** In a mortar and pestle or with the back of a knife, make a paste with the minced garlic and a pinch of salt. This helps to mellow the raw garlic flavor.
4. **Combine the Garlic and Potatoes:** Add the garlic paste to the mashed potatoes and mix well.
5. **Add Olive Oil and Vinegar/Lemon Juice:** Gradually drizzle in the extra-virgin olive oil while continuing to mix. The mixture should become creamy and smooth. Next, add the white wine vinegar or fresh lemon juice, starting with 2 tablespoons, and adjust to taste. Continue mixing until the skordalia is well combined.
6. **Season:** Season the skordalia with additional salt and freshly ground black pepper to taste. You can also adjust the acidity by adding more vinegar or lemon juice if needed.
7. **Chill:** Cover the skordalia and refrigerate for at least 1 hour before serving. Chilling allows the flavors to meld together and enhances the taste.
8. **Serve:** When serving, drizzle a bit of extra-virgin olive oil over the top of the skordalia. Garnish with chopped fresh parsley and Kalamata olives if desired.
9. **Enjoy:** Skordalia can be served as a dip with warm pita bread, slices of cucumber, or other fresh vegetables. It also pairs wonderfully with grilled meats or fish.

Fried Calamari

Ingredients:

For the Calamari:

- 1 pound (450g) cleaned squid tubes and tentacles, cut into rings
- 1 cup all-purpose flour, for dredging
- 1 teaspoon salt
- 1/2 teaspoon black pepper
- 1/2 teaspoon paprika (optional, for added flavor)
- Vegetable oil, for frying
- Lemon wedges, for serving

For the Marinara Sauce (Optional):

- 1 cup tomato sauce or crushed tomatoes
- 2 cloves garlic, minced
- 1/2 teaspoon dried oregano
- Salt and black pepper, to taste
- Crushed red pepper flakes (optional, for heat)

Instructions:

For the Marinara Sauce (Optional):

1. In a small saucepan, heat a bit of olive oil over medium heat. Add the minced garlic and sauté for about 1 minute until fragrant.
2. Add the tomato sauce or crushed tomatoes to the saucepan. Stir in the dried oregano and season with salt, black pepper, and crushed red pepper flakes to taste.
3. Simmer the sauce for about 10-15 minutes, stirring occasionally. Taste and adjust the seasoning as needed. Keep the marinara sauce warm while you prepare the fried calamari.

For the Fried Calamari:

1. In a bowl, combine the all-purpose flour, salt, black pepper, and paprika (if using).
2. Heat vegetable oil in a deep frying pan or a large heavy-bottomed pot to 350-375°F (175-190°C). You'll need enough oil to submerge the calamari rings.
3. While the oil is heating, gently toss the calamari rings in the flour mixture to coat them evenly. Shake off any excess flour.
4. Carefully add the calamari rings to the hot oil in batches, making sure not to overcrowd the pan. Fry them for about 1-2 minutes, or until they turn golden brown and crispy.
5. Use a slotted spoon or tongs to remove the fried calamari from the oil and place them on a plate lined with paper towels to drain any excess oil.
6. Continue frying the remaining batches of calamari until all are cooked.
7. Serve the hot fried calamari immediately with lemon wedges for squeezing and the optional marinara sauce for dipping.

Arancini

Ingredients:

For the Risotto:

- 1 cup Arborio rice
- 4 cups chicken or vegetable broth
- 1 small onion, finely chopped
- 2 tablespoons butter
- 1/2 cup dry white wine (optional)
- 1/2 cup grated Parmesan cheese
- Salt and black pepper, to taste

For the Filling (Suggested: Mozzarella and Peas):

- 1/2 cup mozzarella cheese, cut into small cubes
- 1/4 cup cooked peas (fresh or frozen)
- Salt and black pepper, to taste

For Breading and Frying:

- 2-3 cups breadcrumbs (Italian-style breadcrumbs work well)
- 2-3 large eggs, beaten
- Vegetable oil, for frying

Instructions:

For the Risotto:

1. In a saucepan, heat the chicken or vegetable broth over medium heat until it simmers. Reduce the heat to low to keep it warm while you prepare the risotto.
2. In a separate large saucepan or deep skillet, melt the butter over medium heat. Add the finely chopped onion and sauté until it becomes translucent, about 2-3 minutes.
3. Add the Arborio rice to the skillet and stir to coat it with the melted butter. Cook for an additional 2-3 minutes, allowing the rice to toast slightly.
4. If using, pour in the dry white wine and cook until it's mostly absorbed by the rice, stirring frequently.
5. Begin adding the warm chicken or vegetable broth, one ladleful at a time, stirring constantly. Wait until each ladleful of broth is mostly absorbed by the rice before adding more. Continue this process until the rice is creamy and cooked al dente. This should take about 18-20 minutes.
6. Stir in the grated Parmesan cheese, salt, and black pepper. Remove the risotto from heat and let it cool for about 15 minutes.

For Assembling the Arancini:

1. Take a small portion of the cooled risotto in your hand and flatten it. Place a cube of mozzarella cheese and a few cooked peas in the center.
2. Encase the filling with the risotto, shaping it into a ball. Ensure the filling is completely covered and the arancini is well-sealed.
3. Repeat this process with the remaining risotto and filling ingredients.

For Breading and Frying:

1. Dip each arancino into the beaten eggs, making sure it's well-coated.
2. Roll the egg-coated arancino in breadcrumbs, covering it evenly.
3. Heat vegetable oil in a deep fryer or a deep, heavy-bottomed pot to 350°F (175°C).
4. Carefully place the arancini in the hot oil, a few at a time, and fry until they turn golden brown and crispy on all sides. This should take about 2-3 minutes. Use a slotted spoon to remove them from the oil and drain on paper towels.
5. Serve the arancini hot, either as an appetizer or a snack. They're delicious on their own or with a side of marinara sauce for dipping.

Bruschetta

Ingredients:

- 4-6 ripe Roma tomatoes, diced
- 2-3 cloves garlic, minced
- 1/4 cup fresh basil leaves, chopped
- 2 tablespoons extra-virgin olive oil
- 1 teaspoon balsamic vinegar
- Salt and freshly ground black pepper, to taste
- 1 baguette or Italian bread, sliced into 1/2-inch thick rounds
- Olive oil, for brushing
- Optional: Grated Parmesan cheese for garnish

Instructions:

1. **Prepare the Tomato Mixture:** In a bowl, combine the diced tomatoes, minced garlic, chopped fresh basil, extra-virgin olive oil, and balsamic vinegar. Season with salt and freshly ground black pepper to taste. Gently toss the ingredients together until well combined. Allow the mixture to sit at room temperature for about 15-20 minutes to allow the flavors to meld.
2. **Preheat the Grill or Oven:** Preheat your grill or oven to medium-high heat (about 400°F/200°C). If using the oven, you can also use a broiler.
3. **Brush the Bread:** Brush both sides of the bread slices with a bit of olive oil. This will help them become crispy when toasted.
4. **Toast the Bread:** Place the bread slices on the grill or in the oven. Grill or toast for about 1-2 minutes per side, or until they are golden brown and have grill marks or are crispy.
5. **Rub with Garlic:** While the bread is still warm, rub each slice with a peeled garlic clove. This imparts a subtle garlic flavor to the bread.
6. **Serve:** Arrange the toasted bread slices on a platter. Give the tomato mixture a final toss, then spoon it generously over each slice of bread.
7. **Garnish:** If desired, sprinkle some grated Parmesan cheese over the top of the bruschetta for added flavor.
8. **Serve Immediately:** Serve the bruschetta immediately while the bread is still warm and crispy. It's a delightful appetizer that's perfect for gatherings or as a light snack.

Caprese Salad

Ingredients:

- 4-6 ripe tomatoes (preferably vine-ripened or heirloom), sliced into 1/4-inch thick rounds
- 8 ounces (about 1 cup) fresh mozzarella cheese, sliced into 1/4-inch thick rounds
- 1 bunch fresh basil leaves
- Extra-virgin olive oil, for drizzling
- Balsamic vinegar, for drizzling (optional)
- Salt and freshly ground black pepper, to taste
- Optional: Balsamic glaze for drizzling

Instructions:

1. **Prepare the Tomato and Mozzarella Slices:**
   - Wash and slice the tomatoes and fresh mozzarella cheese into rounds that are approximately 1/4-inch thick. Try to make the slices as uniform as possible for a visually appealing presentation.
2. **Assemble the Caprese Salad:**
   - On a large serving platter, arrange the tomato slices and mozzarella slices in an alternating pattern. Overlap them slightly for an attractive display.
3. **Add Fresh Basil:**
   - Tuck fresh basil leaves between the tomato and mozzarella slices. You can use whole leaves or tear them into smaller pieces.
4. **Season with Salt and Pepper:**
   - Season the salad with a pinch of salt and freshly ground black pepper to taste. Be conservative with the salt, as the cheese can be salty.
5. **Drizzle with Olive Oil:**
   - Drizzle extra-virgin olive oil generously over the top of the salad. Use good-quality olive oil for the best flavor.
6. **Optional Balsamic Vinegar or Glaze:**
   - If desired, you can also drizzle a small amount of balsamic vinegar over the salad for a sweet and tangy contrast. Alternatively, you can use balsamic glaze for a thicker and sweeter drizzle.
7. **Serve Immediately:**
   - Caprese salad is best enjoyed fresh and at room temperature. Serve it immediately as an appetizer or side dish.
8. **Variations:**
   - Feel free to customize your Caprese salad by adding extras like toasted pine nuts, olives, or a sprinkle of Italian seasoning.

Melitzanosalata

Ingredients:

- 2 large eggplants (about 1.5 to 2 pounds)
- 2-3 cloves garlic, minced
- 2 tablespoons tahini (sesame paste)
- 1/4 cup extra-virgin olive oil, plus more for drizzling
- Juice of 1 lemon (about 3-4 tablespoons)
- 2 tablespoons chopped fresh parsley, for garnish
- Salt and black pepper, to taste
- Optional: a pinch of paprika or red pepper flakes for a touch of heat

Instructions:

1. **Roast the Eggplants:**
   - Preheat your oven to 400°F (200°C). Prick the eggplants with a fork in several places to prevent them from bursting during roasting.
   - Place the whole eggplants on a baking sheet lined with parchment paper or aluminum foil. Roast them in the preheated oven for about 45 minutes to 1 hour, or until they become tender and the skin is charred, turning them occasionally for even cooking.
   - Remove the eggplants from the oven and let them cool for a few minutes.

2. **Peel and Drain:**
   - Once the eggplants are cool enough to handle, peel off the charred skin. It should come off easily.
   - Place the peeled eggplants in a colander or fine-mesh strainer to drain excess liquid for about 15-20 minutes.

3. **Blend the Ingredients:**
   - In a food processor or blender, combine the roasted eggplant flesh, minced garlic, tahini, extra-virgin olive oil, and lemon juice. Blend until the mixture is smooth and creamy. You may need to stop and scrape down the sides of the bowl as needed.

4. **Season and Garnish:**
   - Season the melitzanosalata with salt and black pepper to taste. If you like a bit of heat, you can also add a pinch of paprika or red pepper flakes.
   - Taste and adjust the seasoning, lemon juice, or tahini if needed to achieve your desired flavor.

5. **Chill and Serve:**
   - Transfer the melitzanosalata to a serving bowl, drizzle with a bit of extra-virgin olive oil, and garnish with chopped fresh parsley.
   - Cover and refrigerate for at least 1 hour before serving to allow the flavors to meld.

6. **Serve:** Serve melitzanosalata as a dip with pita bread, crusty bread, or fresh vegetables. It's also a great accompaniment to grilled meats and fish.

Marinated Artichoke Hearts

Ingredients:

- 1 can (about 14 ounces) artichoke hearts, drained and quartered (or you can use frozen or fresh artichoke hearts, prepared and cooked)
- 2 cloves garlic, minced
- 1/4 cup extra-virgin olive oil
- 2 tablespoons white wine vinegar or red wine vinegar
- 1/2 teaspoon dried oregano
- 1/2 teaspoon dried basil
- 1/4 teaspoon red pepper flakes (adjust to taste for heat)
- Salt and black pepper, to taste
- Zest of 1 lemon (optional, for added flavor)
- Chopped fresh parsley, for garnish (optional)

Instructions:

1. **Prepare the Artichoke Hearts:**
   - If you're using canned artichoke hearts, drain them and quarter them. If using fresh or frozen artichoke hearts, make sure they are cooked and tender. If not, you may need to boil or steam them according to the package instructions before using.
2. **Make the Marinade:**
   - In a bowl, whisk together the minced garlic, extra-virgin olive oil, white wine vinegar or red wine vinegar, dried oregano, dried basil, red pepper flakes, and a pinch of salt and black pepper. Add the lemon zest if desired for added flavor.
3. **Marinate the Artichoke Hearts:**
   - Place the quartered artichoke hearts in a shallow dish or a glass container with a lid.
   - Pour the marinade over the artichoke hearts, making sure they are well coated. You can use a spoon to gently toss them in the marinade.
4. **Chill and Marinate:**
   - Cover the dish or container and refrigerate the marinated artichoke hearts for at least 2 hours, or ideally overnight. This allows the flavors to infuse into the artichoke hearts.
5. **Serve:**
   - Before serving, let the marinated artichoke hearts come to room temperature. Sprinkle with chopped fresh parsley for a garnish if desired.
   - Serve them as an appetizer, as a topping for salads or pasta, or as a flavorful addition to antipasto platters.
6. **Storage:**
   - Leftover marinated artichoke hearts can be stored in the refrigerator in an airtight container for several days.

Shrimp Cocktail

Ingredients:

For the Shrimp:

- 1 pound large shrimp, peeled and deveined (with tails left on, if desired)
- 1 lemon, sliced
- 1 bay leaf
- Salt, to taste
- Ice water (for an ice bath)

For the Cocktail Sauce:

- 1/2 cup ketchup
- 2 tablespoons prepared horseradish sauce (adjust to taste)
- 1 tablespoon fresh lemon juice
- 1 teaspoon Worcestershire sauce
- A few dashes of hot sauce (e.g., Tabasco), to taste
- Salt and freshly ground black pepper, to taste

For Garnish (Optional):

- Fresh lemon wedges
- Fresh parsley sprigs
- Celery sticks or cucumber slices

Instructions:

For the Shrimp:

1. Fill a large pot with water and add lemon slices, a bay leaf, and a pinch of salt. Bring the water to a boil.
2. Add the shrimp to the boiling water and cook for about 2-3 minutes or until the shrimp turn pink and opaque. Be careful not to overcook them, as they can become tough.
3. Quickly remove the shrimp from the boiling water and immediately transfer them to a bowl of ice water to stop the cooking process. This will help the shrimp cool down rapidly and maintain their texture.
4. Once the shrimp are cooled, drain them and refrigerate until ready to serve.

For the Cocktail Sauce:

1. In a small bowl, combine the ketchup, prepared horseradish sauce, fresh lemon juice, Worcestershire sauce, and hot sauce. Mix well to combine.
2. Taste the cocktail sauce and adjust the seasoning by adding more horseradish sauce, lemon juice, hot sauce, salt, or pepper to suit your preference. It should have a balanced flavor of sweetness, tanginess, and spiciness.

To Assemble:

1. Arrange the chilled shrimp on a serving platter. You can place them around the edge of the platter with a central bowl of cocktail sauce.
2. Garnish the platter with fresh lemon wedges, parsley sprigs, and celery sticks or cucumber slices, if desired.
3. Serve the shrimp cocktail with the cocktail sauce on the side for dipping.
4. Enjoy your homemade shrimp cocktail as an elegant appetizer!

Stuffed Mushrooms

Ingredients:

- 20-24 large white button mushrooms
- 8 ounces (about 1 cup) cream cheese, softened
- 1/2 cup grated Parmesan cheese
- 2 cloves garlic, minced
- 2 tablespoons fresh parsley, finely chopped
- 1/2 teaspoon dried oregano
- Salt and black pepper, to taste
- 2-3 tablespoons breadcrumbs (optional, for topping)
- Olive oil, for brushing
- Fresh parsley or chives, for garnish (optional)

Instructions:

1. **Prepare the Mushrooms:**
   - Preheat your oven to 350°F (175°C).
   - Clean the mushrooms using a damp cloth or paper towel to remove any dirt. Remove the stems by gently twisting them or using a small spoon to scoop them out. Reserve the mushroom caps and finely chop the stems.
2. **Prepare the Filling:**
   - In a mixing bowl, combine the softened cream cheese, grated Parmesan cheese, minced garlic, chopped fresh parsley, dried oregano, salt, and black pepper. Mix until all the ingredients are well combined.
   - Add the chopped mushroom stems to the filling mixture and mix them in as well.
3. **Stuff the Mushrooms:**
   - Using a small spoon or your fingers, stuff each mushroom cap generously with the cream cheese mixture. Mound the filling on top, and if desired, you can press it gently to compact it.
4. **Optional Breadcrumb Topping:**
   - If you'd like to add a crispy topping to your stuffed mushrooms, you can sprinkle breadcrumbs lightly over each stuffed mushroom.
5. **Brush with Olive Oil:**
   - Place the stuffed mushrooms on a baking sheet or in a baking dish. Lightly brush the tops of the mushrooms with olive oil.
6. **Bake:**
   - Bake the stuffed mushrooms in the preheated oven for about 20-25 minutes, or until the mushrooms are tender and the filling is golden brown and slightly bubbly.
7. **Garnish and Serve:**
   - Remove the stuffed mushrooms from the oven and let them cool for a few minutes before serving.
   - Garnish with fresh parsley or chives, if desired.
8. **Serve Warm:**
   - Stuffed mushrooms are best served warm. Enjoy them as a delicious appetizer for your next gathering!

Grilled Halloumi

Ingredients:

- 8 ounces (about 1/2 pound) halloumi cheese, sliced into 1/4-inch thick pieces
- 1-2 tablespoons olive oil, for brushing
- Fresh lemon wedges, for serving
- Fresh herbs (such as mint, basil, or parsley), for garnish (optional)

Instructions:

1. **Preheat the Grill:**
   - Preheat your grill to medium-high heat (around 400-450°F or 200-230°C). Make sure the grill grates are clean and lightly oiled to prevent the cheese from sticking.
2. **Prepare the Halloumi:**
   - Slice the halloumi cheese into approximately 1/4-inch thick slices. You can cut it into rectangles or triangles, depending on your preference.
3. **Brush with Olive Oil:**
   - Lightly brush both sides of each halloumi slice with olive oil. This will help prevent sticking and create a nice grill mark.
4. **Grill the Halloumi:**
   - Place the halloumi slices directly on the preheated grill. Grill them for about 1-2 minutes per side, or until you see grill marks and the cheese starts to become slightly crispy on the outside.
   - Be careful not to overcook the halloumi; it should be golden brown with grill marks but still soft and slightly creamy on the inside.
5. **Serve Hot:**
   - Remove the grilled halloumi from the grill and transfer it to a serving platter.
6. **Garnish and Serve:**
   - Squeeze fresh lemon juice over the grilled halloumi slices for added flavor. You can also garnish with fresh herbs like mint, basil, or parsley if desired.
7. **Serve Immediately:**
   - Grilled halloumi is best enjoyed hot and fresh from the grill. Serve it as an appetizer, part of a mezze platter, or as a topping for salads or sandwiches.

Patatas Bravas

Ingredients:

For the Potatoes:

- 4-5 medium russet potatoes, peeled and cut into 1-inch cubes
- Vegetable oil, for frying
- Salt, to taste

For the Spicy Tomato Sauce (Salsa Brava):

- 1 can (14 ounces) diced tomatoes
- 2 cloves garlic, minced
- 1 teaspoon paprika (sweet or smoked)
- 1/2 teaspoon cayenne pepper (adjust to taste for heat)
- Salt and black pepper, to taste
- Olive oil, for sautéing

For the Garlic Aioli:

- 1/2 cup mayonnaise
- 2 cloves garlic, minced
- 1 tablespoon fresh lemon juice
- Salt and black pepper, to taste

Instructions:

For the Potatoes:

1. **Fry the Potatoes:**
   - Heat vegetable oil in a deep frying pan or a pot to 350°F (175°C).
   - Carefully add the potato cubes to the hot oil in batches to avoid overcrowding. Fry them until they are golden and crispy, which should take about 5-7 minutes per batch.
   - Remove the fried potatoes using a slotted spoon and transfer them to a plate lined with paper towels to drain excess oil. Season with salt while they are still hot.

For the Spicy Tomato Sauce (Salsa Brava):

1. **Sauté the Garlic:** In a saucepan, heat a bit of olive oil over medium heat. Add the minced garlic and sauté for about 1-2 minutes, or until fragrant.
2. **Add Tomatoes and Spices:** Add the diced tomatoes, paprika, cayenne pepper, salt, and black pepper to the saucepan. Stir to combine.
3. **Simmer:** Allow the sauce to simmer over low to medium heat for about 15-20 minutes, or until it thickens and the flavors meld. Stir occasionally.
4. **Blend (Optional):** If you prefer a smoother sauce, you can use an immersion blender or a regular blender to blend the sauce until it's smooth.

For the Garlic Aioli:

1. **Prepare the Aioli:** In a small bowl, combine the mayonnaise, minced garlic, fresh lemon juice, salt, and black pepper. Mix until well combined.

To Serve Patatas Bravas:

1. **Arrange the Potatoes:** Place the crispy fried potato cubes on a serving platter.
2. **Drizzle with Sauce:** Spoon the spicy tomato sauce (Salsa Brava) over the fried potatoes. You can be as generous as you like.
3. **Add Garlic Aioli:** Drizzle the garlic aioli over the top of the potatoes or serve it on the side for dipping.
4. **Garnish:** Optionally, garnish the dish with chopped fresh parsley for color and freshness.
5. **Serve Hot:** Patatas Bravas are best served hot as a tapas dish or appetizer. Enjoy!

Crab Cakes

Ingredients:

- 1 pound lump crab meat, picked over to remove any shells
- 1/3 cup mayonnaise
- 1 large egg
- 1 tablespoon Dijon mustard
- 1 tablespoon Worcestershire sauce
- 1/4 cup finely chopped green onions (green parts only)
- 1/4 cup finely chopped red bell pepper
- 1/4 cup finely chopped celery
- 1 1/2 cups breadcrumbs (divided)
- 1/4 cup fresh parsley, chopped
- 1 teaspoon Old Bay seasoning (or more to taste)
- 1/4 teaspoon cayenne pepper (optional, for heat)
- Salt and black pepper, to taste
- Vegetable oil, for frying

Instructions:

1. **Prepare the Crab Meat:**
   - Carefully pick through the crab meat to remove any shells or cartilage. Be gentle to keep the crab meat in large chunks.
2. **Mix the Crab Cake Ingredients:**
   - In a large bowl, combine the mayonnaise, egg, Dijon mustard, Worcestershire sauce, green onions, red bell pepper, celery, 1/2 cup of breadcrumbs, parsley, Old Bay seasoning, and cayenne pepper (if using). Season with salt and black pepper to taste.
3. **Gently Fold in the Crab Meat:**
   - Gently fold the lump crab meat into the mixture, being careful not to break up the crab meat too much. The mixture should be moist but hold together.
4. **Form the Crab Cakes:**
   - Use your hands to form the mixture into 8 equal-sized crab cakes. Shape them into patties about 1 inch thick. Place the remaining 1 cup of breadcrumbs in a shallow dish.
5. **Coat with Breadcrumbs:**
   - Carefully coat each crab cake with breadcrumbs, pressing them lightly onto the surface of the cakes to help them adhere.
6. **Chill the Crab Cakes:**
   - Place the crab cakes on a baking sheet and refrigerate for at least 30 minutes. Chilling them helps them hold their shape while cooking.
7. **Fry the Crab Cakes:**
   - Heat about 1/4 inch of vegetable oil in a large skillet over medium-high heat. Once hot, carefully add the crab cakes and cook for about 3-4 minutes on each side, or until they are golden brown and heated through.
8. **Drain and Serve:**
   - Place the cooked crab cakes on a plate lined with paper towels to drain any excess oil.

Mussels in White Wine Sauce

Ingredients:

- 2 pounds fresh mussels, cleaned and debearded
- 2 tablespoons olive oil
- 1 small onion, finely chopped
- 2 cloves garlic, minced
- 1/2 cup dry white wine (such as Sauvignon Blanc)
- 1/2 cup chicken or vegetable broth
- 1/2 cup heavy cream (or substitute with half-and-half for a lighter sauce)
- 2-3 tablespoons fresh parsley, chopped
- Salt and black pepper, to taste
- Red pepper flakes (optional, for heat)
- Crusty bread or French fries, for serving

Instructions:

1. **Clean the Mussels:**
   - Scrub and clean the mussels under cold running water, removing any beards and discarding any mussels that are open or damaged.
2. **Prepare the Ingredients:**
   - Finely chop the onion, mince the garlic, and chop the fresh parsley.
3. **Sauté the Aromatics:**
   - In a large, deep skillet or a Dutch oven, heat the olive oil over medium heat. Add the chopped onion and sauté for about 2-3 minutes until it becomes soft and translucent.
4. **Add Garlic and Wine:**
   - Add the minced garlic to the skillet and sauté for another 30 seconds to 1 minute until fragrant.
   - Pour in the dry white wine and bring it to a simmer. Cook for 2-3 minutes, allowing the alcohol to cook off and the wine to reduce slightly.
5. **Add Mussels:**
   - Carefully add the cleaned mussels to the skillet. Give them a gentle stir to combine them with the wine and onion mixture.
6. **Simmer and Cover:**
   - Pour in the chicken or vegetable broth and cover the skillet. Allow the mussels to simmer for about 4-5 minutes, or until they open. Discard any mussels that remain closed after cooking.
7. **Add Cream and Seasoning:**
   - Reduce the heat to low, and pour in the heavy cream (or half-and-half). Stir to combine with the broth and wine.
   - Season the sauce with salt and black pepper to taste. If you like a little heat, you can also add a pinch of red pepper flakes.
8. **Garnish and Serve:**
   - Sprinkle the chopped fresh parsley over the mussels and sauce. Give it a final gentle stir.
9. **Serve:**
   - Serve the mussels in white wine sauce in deep bowls. They are best enjoyed with crusty bread or French fries to soak up the delicious broth.

Chorizo in Red Wine

Ingredients:

- 6-8 links of spicy chorizo sausage
- 1 bottle (750ml) of dry red wine (such as Rioja or Tempranillo)
- 2-3 cloves of garlic, minced
- 1 small onion, finely chopped
- 1 bay leaf
- 1 teaspoon paprika (smoked or sweet)
- 1 teaspoon dried oregano
- 1/2 teaspoon cayenne pepper (adjust to taste for heat)
- Salt and black pepper, to taste
- Olive oil, for sautéing
- Fresh parsley, for garnish (optional)
- Crusty bread or baguette, for serving

Instructions:

1. **Prepare the Chorizo:**
   - If the chorizo sausages are in a casing, you can leave them whole or slice them into 1-inch pieces, depending on your preference.
2. **Sauté the Chorizo:**
   - In a large skillet or frying pan, heat a bit of olive oil over medium-high heat. Add the chorizo sausages and cook them for about 3-4 minutes on each side, or until they are browned and slightly crispy.
3. **Remove Chorizo:**
   - Once the chorizo is cooked, transfer them to a plate and set them aside.
4. **Sauté Onion and Garlic:**
   - In the same skillet, add a little more olive oil if needed. Add the minced garlic and chopped onion. Sauté for about 2-3 minutes until the onion becomes soft and translucent.
5. **Add Wine and Seasonings:**
   - Return the cooked chorizo to the skillet. Pour in the entire bottle of red wine, and add the bay leaf, paprika, dried oregano, and cayenne pepper. Season with salt and black pepper to taste.
6. **Simmer:**
   - Allow the mixture to come to a simmer. Reduce the heat to low and let it simmer for about 20-30 minutes. The wine will reduce and thicken, creating a flavorful sauce.
7. **Serve:**
   - Remove the bay leaf and discard it. Sprinkle with fresh parsley, if desired.
   - Serve the Chorizo in Red Wine in a deep serving dish or individual small plates. It's traditionally served with crusty bread or baguette to soak up the delicious wine sauce.

Tomato and Mozzarella Skewers

Ingredients:

- Cherry tomatoes (you'll need about 20-24)
- Fresh mini mozzarella balls (also known as bocconcini)
- Fresh basil leaves
- Extra-virgin olive oil
- Balsamic glaze or balsamic reduction (optional)
- Salt and freshly ground black pepper, to taste
- Toothpicks or small skewers

Instructions:

1. **Prepare the Ingredients:**
   - Wash and dry the cherry tomatoes and fresh basil leaves.
   - Drain the mini mozzarella balls.
2. **Assemble the Skewers:**
   - Start by skewering a cherry tomato, followed by a folded basil leaf, and then a mozzarella ball onto each toothpick or small skewer. The order is flexible, so you can arrange them to your preference.
3. **Drizzle with Olive Oil:**
   - Arrange the assembled skewers on a serving platter. Drizzle extra-virgin olive oil over the skewers, allowing it to coat the ingredients.
4. **Season with Salt and Pepper:**
   - Sprinkle the skewers with a pinch of salt and freshly ground black pepper to taste.
5. **Optional Balsamic Glaze:**
   - If you like, you can add a touch of balsamic glaze or balsamic reduction for a sweet and tangy flavor. Drizzle it over the skewers as a final touch.
6. **Serve:**
   - Serve the tomato and mozzarella skewers immediately. They make for a refreshing and colorful appetizer that's perfect for gatherings or as a light snack.

Taramasalata

Ingredients:

- 1/2 cup tarama (fish roe)
- 2-3 slices of day-old white bread, crusts removed
- 2 cloves garlic, minced
- 1/4 cup extra-virgin olive oil
- Juice of 1 lemon
- 2-3 tablespoons red or white wine vinegar (adjust to taste)
- 1/4 cup cold water (or more as needed)
- Salt and freshly ground black pepper, to taste
- Optional: 1 small boiled potato, mashed (to add creaminess)

Instructions:

1. **Soak the Bread:**
   - Start by soaking the slices of day-old white bread in a small bowl of cold water for a few minutes, until they become soggy.
2. **Prepare the Tarama:**
   - In another bowl, mix the tarama with lemon juice and vinegar until it forms a smooth paste. This can be a bit challenging and may take some time, so be patient. You can also use a food processor to help blend the tarama.
3. **Blend the Ingredients:**
   - Squeeze the excess water from the soaked bread and add the bread to the tarama mixture.
   - Add the minced garlic and optional mashed potato for creaminess.
   - Begin blending the mixture while gradually drizzling in the olive oil. Continue blending until it becomes a smooth and creamy paste.
4. **Adjust the Consistency:**
   - If the Taramasalata is too thick, you can add cold water a little at a time until you reach your desired consistency. Some prefer it thicker, while others like it creamier.
5. **Season and Serve:**
   - Season with salt and freshly ground black pepper to taste. Taste the Taramasalata and adjust the lemon juice, vinegar, or salt as needed to suit your preference.
6. **Chill:**
   - Transfer the Taramasalata to a bowl, cover it, and refrigerate for at least an hour before serving. This allows the flavors to meld and develop.
7. **Serve:**
   - Serve Taramasalata as a dip with pita bread, crackers, or fresh vegetables. You can also drizzle a bit of olive oil and garnish with fresh herbs or paprika for added flavor and presentation.

Pide

Ingredients:

For the Dough:
- 2 1/4 teaspoons (1 packet) active dry yeast
- 1 teaspoon sugar
- 1 cup warm water
- 2 1/2 to 3 cups all-purpose flour
- 1 teaspoon salt

For the Filling:
- 1/2 pound ground beef or lamb
- 1 small onion, finely chopped
- 2 cloves garlic, minced
- 1 teaspoon ground cumin
- 1 teaspoon ground paprika
- Salt and black pepper, to taste
- 1 tablespoon tomato paste
- 2 tablespoons olive oil

For Topping:
- 1-2 tomatoes, sliced
- 1/2 cup grated mozzarella or feta cheese (optional)
- 1 egg (for egg wash)
- Optional: Black olives, green peppers, or other desired toppings

Instructions:

Prepare the Dough:
1. In a small bowl, combine the active dry yeast, sugar, and warm water. Let it sit for about 5-10 minutes, or until it becomes frothy.
2. In a large mixing bowl, combine 2 1/2 cups of all-purpose flour and salt. Pour in the yeast mixture and mix until a soft, slightly sticky dough forms. If needed, add a little more flour, one tablespoon at a time, until the dough is manageable.
3. Knead the dough for about 5-7 minutes until it's smooth and elastic. Place it in a lightly oiled bowl, cover with a damp cloth, and let it rise in a warm place for about 1-2 hours, or until it has doubled in size.

Prepare the Filling:
1. In a skillet, heat 2 tablespoons of olive oil over medium heat. Add the chopped onion and garlic and sauté until they become soft and translucent.
2. Add the ground meat to the skillet and cook until browned. Break it up with a spoon as it cooks.
3. Stir in the tomato paste, cumin, paprika, salt, and black pepper. Cook for a few more minutes, allowing the flavors to meld. Remove from heat and set aside.

Assemble the Pide:
1. Preheat your oven to 450°F (230°C) and place a pizza stone or baking sheet in the oven to heat.
2. Punch down the risen dough and divide it into 4 equal portions.
3. On a lightly floured surface, roll out each portion into an oval shape, about 1/4-inch thick.
4. Transfer the rolled-out dough to a piece of parchment paper.
5. Spread the meat filling on each piece of dough, leaving a border around the edges.
6. Arrange the sliced tomatoes and optional toppings on the filling.
7. Fold the edges of the dough over the filling, pinching and folding to create the boat shape of the Pide.
8. Beat the egg and brush it over the edges of the Pide for a shiny finish.
9. Slide the parchment paper with the Pide onto the hot pizza stone or baking sheet in the oven.
10. Bake for about 15-20 minutes or until the Pide is golden brown and the edges are crisp.
11. Remove from the oven and let it cool for a few minutes before slicing.
12. Serve your homemade Pide while it's still warm. Enjoy!

Zucchini

Ingredients:

- 2 medium zucchinis (about 2 cups grated)
- 1 teaspoon salt
- 1/2 cup all-purpose flour
- 1/2 cup grated Parmesan cheese
- 1/4 cup finely chopped fresh herbs (such as dill, parsley, or mint)
- 2 cloves garlic, minced
- 1/4 cup finely chopped green onions (optional)
- 2 large eggs, beaten
- Black pepper, to taste
- Olive oil, for frying

Instructions:

1. **Prepare the Zucchini:**
   - Grate the zucchinis using a box grater or a food processor with the grating attachment.
2. **Drain the Zucchini:**
   - Place the grated zucchini in a colander, sprinkle with 1 teaspoon of salt, and let it sit for about 10-15 minutes. The salt will help release excess moisture from the zucchini.
3. **Squeeze Out Excess Moisture:**
   - After the resting time, use your hands to squeeze and press the grated zucchini to remove as much liquid as possible. You can also place the zucchini in a clean kitchen towel and twist it to wring out the moisture.
4. **Mix the Ingredients:**
   - In a large mixing bowl, combine the grated and drained zucchini, all-purpose flour, grated Parmesan cheese, minced garlic, finely chopped herbs, and green onions (if using). Mix everything together.
5. **Add Eggs and Season:**
   - Add the beaten eggs to the mixture and season with black pepper. Stir until all the ingredients are well combined. The mixture should be thick and sticky.
6. **Heat Olive Oil:**
   - In a large skillet, heat a generous amount of olive oil over medium-high heat. You'll want enough oil to cover the bottom of the skillet.
7. **Fry the Fritters:**
   - Once the oil is hot, use a spoon or your hands to form small patties from the zucchini mixture. Carefully place the patties in the hot oil.
8. **Cook Until Golden Brown:**
   - Fry the zucchini fritters for about 2-3 minutes on each side, or until they are golden brown and crispy. You may need to work in batches, depending on the size of your skillet.
9. **Drain and Serve:**
   - Remove the cooked fritters and place them on a plate lined with paper towels to drain any excess oil.
10. **Serve Warm:**
    - Serve the zucchini fritters while they're still warm. They're great on their own or with a dollop of Greek yogurt, sour cream, or a yogurt-based tzatziki sauce for dipping.

Grilled Octopus

Ingredients:

- 2 pounds (approximately 1 kg) octopus, cleaned and tentacles separated
- 1/4 cup extra-virgin olive oil
- Juice of 1-2 lemons
- 4 cloves garlic, minced
- 1-2 teaspoons dried oregano
- Salt and black pepper, to taste
- Lemon wedges, for serving
- Fresh parsley, for garnish

Instructions:

1. **Prepare the Octopus:**
   - If you're using fresh octopus, make sure it's cleaned and the beak (mouth) is removed. If you're using frozen octopus, defrost it completely before cooking.
2. **Parboil the Octopus:**
   - In a large pot, bring water to a boil. Add the octopus and simmer for about 20-30 minutes. Cooking time may vary depending on the size and tenderness of the octopus. It's done when a fork can be easily inserted into the flesh.
3. **Drain and Cool:**
   - Drain the octopus and let it cool to room temperature.
4. **Marinate the Octopus:**
   - In a bowl, combine the olive oil, lemon juice, minced garlic, dried oregano, salt, and black pepper.
5. **Coat the Octopus:**
   - Place the octopus in a shallow dish and pour the marinade over it. Make sure the octopus is well coated. Let it marinate for about 30 minutes to 1 hour.
6. **Preheat the Grill:**
   - Preheat your grill to medium-high heat, around 450°F (230°C). Clean and oil the grill grates to prevent sticking.
7. **Grill the Octopus:**
   - Place the marinated octopus on the grill and cook for about 2-4 minutes on each side, or until it's nicely charred and has grill marks. Baste it with any remaining marinade as it cooks.
8. **Serve:**
   - Transfer the grilled octopus to a serving platter and drizzle any remaining marinade over it. Garnish with fresh parsley and serve with lemon wedges.

Htipiti (Spicy Feta Dip)

Ingredients:

- 8 ounces (about 1 cup) crumbled feta cheese
- 2-3 roasted red bell peppers (you can use jarred roasted peppers or roast them yourself)
- 2 cloves garlic, minced
- 1 tablespoon extra-virgin olive oil
- 1 tablespoon lemon juice
- 1 teaspoon red pepper flakes (adjust to taste for heat)
- 1 teaspoon dried oregano
- Salt and black pepper, to taste
- Fresh parsley, for garnish (optional)
- Olive oil, for drizzling

Instructions:

1. **Roast the Red Peppers (if not using jarred):**
   - Preheat your broiler or grill. Place the red peppers on a baking sheet or grill rack and cook until the skins blister and blacken, turning them occasionally. This should take about 15-20 minutes.
   - Remove the peppers from the heat source, place them in a bowl, and cover them with plastic wrap. Allow them to cool for about 15 minutes.
   - Peel off the skin, remove the seeds and stem, and chop the roasted red peppers into small pieces.
2. **Prepare the Htipiti:**
   - In a food processor, combine the crumbled feta cheese, roasted red peppers, minced garlic, olive oil, lemon juice, red pepper flakes, and dried oregano.
3. **Blend:**
   - Blend the mixture until it's smooth and creamy. You can adjust the consistency by adding more olive oil if needed.
4. **Season and Garnish:**
   - Season the Htipiti with salt and black pepper to taste. Stir to combine.
   - If you like, garnish the dip with chopped fresh parsley for a pop of color and freshness.
5. **Serve:**
   - Transfer the Htipiti to a serving dish. Drizzle a bit of olive oil on top for extra flavor and presentation.
6. **Enjoy:**
   - Htipiti is traditionally served as a dip with pita bread, crackers, or fresh vegetables. It can also be used as a spread for sandwiches or as a condiment for grilled meats and seafood.

Gavurdagi Salad

Ingredients:

- 4 large ripe tomatoes, diced
- 2-3 hot green peppers (such as green chili peppers), finely chopped (adjust to taste for heat)
- 1 small red onion, finely chopped
- 1/2 cup fresh parsley, chopped
- 1/2 cup walnuts, coarsely chopped
- 2-3 tablespoons pomegranate molasses
- 3-4 tablespoons extra-virgin olive oil
- Juice of 1 lemon
- Salt and black pepper, to taste
- Sumac (optional, for garnish)
- Pomegranate seeds (optional, for garnish)

Instructions:

1. **Prepare the Vegetables:**
   - Dice the tomatoes and finely chop the red onion, hot green peppers, and fresh parsley. You can adjust the quantity of green peppers to your preferred level of spiciness.
2. **Combine the Vegetables:**
   - In a large serving bowl, combine the diced tomatoes, chopped red onion, hot green peppers, and fresh parsley.
3. **Add Walnuts:**
   - Add the coarsely chopped walnuts to the bowl. You can lightly toast the walnuts for extra flavor if you prefer.
4. **Prepare the Dressing:**
   - In a small bowl, whisk together the pomegranate molasses, extra-virgin olive oil, and lemon juice until well combined. Season with salt and black pepper to taste.
5. **Toss and Dress:**
   - Drizzle the dressing over the salad ingredients in the bowl.
6. **Mix and Adjust:**
   - Gently toss the salad to combine all the ingredients and coat them with the dressing. Taste and adjust the seasoning, adding more salt, pepper, pomegranate molasses, or lemon juice as needed to achieve your desired flavor balance.
7. **Garnish:**
   - If desired, sprinkle the top of the salad with sumac for extra tang and pomegranate seeds for a burst of color and freshness.
8. **Chill and Serve:**
   - Allow the salad to chill in the refrigerator for about 30 minutes before serving to allow the flavors to meld.
9. **Serve:**
   - Gavurdagi Salad is typically served as a side dish or appetizer. It pairs wonderfully with grilled meats, kebabs, or as a topping for pita bread or flatbreads.

Lahmacun

Ingredients:

For the Dough:

- 2 1/4 teaspoons (1 packet) active dry yeast
- 1 teaspoon sugar
- 1 cup warm water
- 2 1/2 to 3 cups all-purpose flour
- 1 teaspoon salt
- 1 tablespoon olive oil

For the Topping:

- 1/2 pound ground lamb or beef
- 1 medium onion, finely chopped
- 2 cloves garlic, minced
- 2 tablespoons tomato paste
- 1 red bell pepper, finely chopped
- 1 green bell pepper, finely chopped
- 1 small bunch fresh parsley, finely chopped
- 1 teaspoon ground cumin
- 1 teaspoon ground paprika
- 1/2 teaspoon cayenne pepper (adjust to taste for heat)
- Salt and black pepper, to taste
- Olive oil, for brushing

Instructions:

Prepare the Dough:

1. In a small bowl, combine the active dry yeast, sugar, and warm water. Let it sit for about 5-10 minutes until it becomes frothy.
2. In a large mixing bowl, combine 2 1/2 cups of all-purpose flour and salt. Pour in the yeast mixture and the olive oil. Mix until a soft, slightly sticky dough forms. If needed, add a little more flour, one tablespoon at a time, until the dough is manageable.
3. Knead the dough for about 5-7 minutes until it's smooth and elastic. Place it in a lightly oiled bowl, cover with a damp cloth, and let it rise in a warm place for about 1-2 hours, or until it has doubled in size.

Prepare the Topping:

1. In a large skillet, heat a bit of olive oil over medium heat. Add the finely chopped onion and garlic, and sauté for about 2-3 minutes until they become soft and translucent.
2. Add the ground lamb or beef to the skillet and cook until browned, breaking it up with a spoon as it cooks.
3. Stir in the tomato paste, ground cumin, ground paprika, cayenne pepper, salt, and black pepper. Cook for a few more minutes, allowing the flavors to meld. Remove from heat and set aside.

Assemble and Cook Lahmacun:

1. Preheat your oven to 450°F (230°C). If you have a pizza stone, place it in the oven while it's heating.
2. Punch down the risen dough and divide it into 8 equal portions.
3. On a lightly floured surface, roll out each portion into a thin, oval shape, about 1/8-inch thick.
4. Place the rolled-out dough on a piece of parchment paper.
5. Spread a portion of the spiced meat mixture over each dough, leaving a small border around the edges.
6. Transfer the parchment paper with the Lahmacun onto the hot pizza stone or a baking sheet.
7. Bake for about 8-10 minutes or until the Lahmacun is nicely browned and crispy.
8. Remove from the oven and allow it to cool for a minute before slicing.
9. Serve your homemade Lahmacun while it's still warm. It's often garnished with fresh parsley and a squeeze of lemon juice.

Ceviche

Ingredients:

- 1 pound fresh white fish (such as cod, tilapia, or sea bass), shrimp, or a combination of seafood, diced into small pieces
- 1 cup freshly squeezed lime juice (about 8-10 limes)
- 1/2 cup freshly squeezed lemon juice (about 4-5 lemons)
- 1 small red onion, thinly sliced
- 1-2 fresh hot chili peppers (like jalapeños), finely chopped (adjust to taste for heat)
- 1-2 cloves garlic, minced
- 1/2 cup fresh cilantro leaves, chopped
- 1 ripe tomato, diced (seeds and excess liquid removed)
- 1/2 cucumber, peeled and diced
- Salt and black pepper, to taste
- 1-2 tablespoons olive oil (optional)
- Avocado slices (for garnish, optional)
- Tortilla chips or toasted corn nuts (for serving)

Instructions:

1. **Prepare the Seafood:**
   - If using shrimp, peel and devein them, then chop them into bite-sized pieces.
   - If using fish, make sure it's fresh and diced into small, even pieces. You can also use a combination of seafood.
2. **Combine with Citrus Juices:**
   - In a glass or ceramic bowl, place the seafood and cover it with the freshly squeezed lime and lemon juice. Make sure the seafood is fully submerged in the juice. This will "cook" the seafood through a process called denaturation. Stir to ensure even exposure to the citrus juices.
3. **Marinate:**
   - Cover the bowl with plastic wrap and refrigerate. Allow the seafood to marinate in the citrus juices for about 30 minutes to 1 hour. The seafood should change in color from translucent to opaque.
4. **Prepare the Vegetables:**
   - While the seafood is marinating, prepare the vegetables. Thinly slice the red onion, finely chop the chili peppers, mince the garlic, chop the fresh cilantro, dice the tomato, and peel and dice the cucumber.
5. **Drain and Mix:**
   - After marinating, remove the seafood from the citrus juices, draining off the excess liquid. You can save a little juice for later if you want a thinner texture.
   - In a clean bowl, combine the marinated seafood, sliced red onion, chopped chili peppers, minced garlic, chopped cilantro, diced tomato, and cucumber.
6. **Season:**
   - Season the mixture with salt and black pepper to taste. You can also drizzle with olive oil for extra flavor and richness.
7. **Refrigerate and Serve:**
   - Refrigerate the ceviche for at least 15-20 minutes before serving to allow the flavors to meld.
8. **Garnish and Serve:**
   - Serve the ceviche in individual bowls or glasses, garnished with avocado slices if desired. It's commonly served with tortilla chips or toasted corn nuts for scooping and added crunch.

Yaprak Sarma

Ingredients:

For the Grape Leaves:

- 1 jar of preserved grape leaves (about 60-80 leaves) or fresh grape leaves if available
- Boiling water

For the Filling:

- 1 cup long-grain rice (such as Arborio or Jasmine rice)
- 1/2 pound ground beef or lamb (optional)
- 1 large onion, finely chopped
- 2 tablespoons olive oil
- 2 tablespoons tomato paste
- 1/4 cup fresh lemon juice
- 1/4 cup chopped fresh parsley
- 1/4 cup chopped fresh mint
- 1/4 cup chopped fresh dill
- 1 teaspoon ground allspice
- 1 teaspoon ground cinnamon
- Salt and black pepper, to taste

For Cooking:

- 2-3 cups chicken or vegetable broth
- Juice of 2 lemons
- Olive oil, for drizzling

Instructions:

Prepare the Grape Leaves:

1. If you are using preserved grape leaves, remove them from the jar and rinse them under cold water to remove excess salt. If you have fresh grape leaves, blanch them briefly in boiling water and drain to soften them.
2. Place the grape leaves in a bowl, cover them with boiling water, and let them soak for about 10-15 minutes. This will help to soften the leaves further.

Prepare the Filling:

1. In a large skillet, heat 2 tablespoons of olive oil over medium heat. Add the finely chopped onion and sauté until it becomes translucent.
2. If you're using ground meat, add it to the skillet and cook until it's browned, breaking it up with a spoon as it cooks.
3. Stir in the tomato paste, chopped fresh herbs (parsley, mint, dill), lemon juice, ground allspice, ground cinnamon, salt, and black pepper. Cook for a few minutes until the mixture is well combined.
4. Add the rice and stir to coat it with the mixture. Cook for an additional 3-5 minutes.

Roll the Sarma:

1. Take one grape leaf, shiny side down, and place it on a clean surface. Cut off the stem if it's too long.
2. Place a small spoonful of the filling in the center of the leaf. Fold in the sides, then roll it tightly into a cylinder shape. Repeat with the remaining grape leaves and filling.

Cook the Sarma:

1. Line the bottom of a large pot with any torn or unused grape leaves to protect the stuffed leaves from direct contact with the heat.
2. Place the rolled grape leaves in the pot, seam side down, packing them tightly.
3. Pour the chicken or vegetable broth over the grape leaves to cover them. You can add more water if needed.
4. Place a heat-resistant plate or an upside-down heatproof bowl on top of the grape leaves to prevent them from unraveling during cooking.
5. Cover the pot and simmer the Yaprak Sarma over low heat for about 45 minutes to 1 hour, or until the rice is fully cooked and the leaves are tender.

Turkish Sigara Borek

Ingredients:

For the Filling:

- 1 cup feta cheese, crumbled
- 1/2 cup fresh parsley, finely chopped
- 1/4 cup fresh dill, finely chopped (optional)
- 1/4 cup green onions or chives, finely chopped
- Black pepper, to taste

For the Dough:

- 10-12 sheets of phyllo pastry (yufka)
- 1/2 cup unsalted butter, melted
- Vegetable oil, for frying

Instructions:

Prepare the Filling:

1. In a mixing bowl, combine the crumbled feta cheese, finely chopped fresh parsley, dill (if using), and green onions or chives. Add black pepper to taste. Mix well and set the filling aside.

Assemble the Sigara Börek:

1. Lay out one sheet of phyllo pastry on a clean, flat surface. Keep the remaining sheets covered with a damp cloth to prevent them from drying out.
2. Brush the entire sheet with melted butter.
3. Place a small amount of the filling mixture (about 2 tablespoons) in a line along one edge of the phyllo sheet, leaving a little space on the sides.
4. Fold in the sides of the phyllo sheet over the filling, then roll it up tightly, similar to rolling a cigar.
5. Continue this process with the remaining phyllo sheets and filling.

Cook the Sigara Börek:

1. In a large skillet, heat vegetable oil over medium-high heat. The oil should be deep enough to submerge the Sigara Börek completely.
2. Carefully place the Sigara Börek rolls into the hot oil and fry until they are golden brown and crispy, turning them as needed. This should take about 2-3 minutes per roll.
3. Use a slotted spoon to remove the fried Sigara Börek from the oil and drain them on a plate lined with paper towels to remove excess oil.

Serve the Sigara Börek:

1. Serve the Sigara Börek while they're still warm. They can be served as an appetizer, snack, or part of a mezze spread, accompanied by yogurt or a simple tomato and cucumber salad.

Shrimp Saganaki

Ingredients:

- 1 1/2 pounds (about 700g) large shrimp, peeled and deveined
- 2 tablespoons olive oil
- 1 medium onion, finely chopped
- 3 cloves garlic, minced
- 1 red bell pepper, finely chopped
- 1 can (14 ounces) diced tomatoes
- 1/4 cup dry white wine (optional)
- 1 teaspoon dried oregano
- 1/2 teaspoon red pepper flakes (adjust to taste for heat)
- Salt and black pepper, to taste
- 1/2 cup crumbled feta cheese
- Chopped fresh parsley, for garnish
- Crusty bread, for serving

Instructions:

1. **Preheat the Oven:** Preheat your oven to 375°F (190°C).
2. **Prepare the Shrimp:** Pat the shrimp dry with paper towels and season them with a little salt and black pepper.
3. **Sauté the Aromatics:** In a large ovenproof skillet, heat the olive oil over medium-high heat. Add the chopped onion and red bell pepper and sauté for about 5 minutes until they become softened and slightly caramelized.
4. **Add Garlic and Tomatoes:** Stir in the minced garlic and cook for about 30 seconds until fragrant. Add the canned diced tomatoes (with their juices) and stir to combine.
5. **Season and Simmer:** Season the mixture with dried oregano, red pepper flakes, salt, and black pepper. If you're using wine, pour it into the skillet and let it simmer for a couple of minutes to reduce.
6. **Cook the Shrimp:** Add the seasoned shrimp to the skillet and cook for about 2-3 minutes on each side, or until they turn pink and start to curl. Be careful not to overcook them, as they will continue cooking in the oven.
7. **Top with Feta:** Sprinkle the crumbled feta cheese over the shrimp and sauce in the skillet.
8. **Bake:** Transfer the skillet to the preheated oven and bake for about 10-15 minutes, or until the cheese is bubbly and slightly browned.
9. **Garnish and Serve:** Remove the skillet from the oven, garnish the Shrimp Saganaki with chopped fresh parsley, and serve hot with crusty bread for dipping.

Stuffed Bell Peppers

Ingredients:

- 4 large bell peppers (any color you prefer)
- 1 pound (450g) ground beef
- 1 cup cooked rice (white or brown)
- 1/2 cup diced onion
- 2 cloves garlic, minced
- 1 can (14 ounces) diced tomatoes
- 1 teaspoon dried oregano
- 1 teaspoon dried basil
- 1/2 teaspoon paprika
- Salt and black pepper, to taste
- 1 cup shredded mozzarella cheese (or your favorite cheese)
- Olive oil, for cooking
- Fresh parsley or basil, for garnish (optional)

Instructions:

1. **Preheat the Oven:** Preheat your oven to 375°F (190°C).
2. **Prepare the Bell Peppers:**
   - Cut the tops off the bell peppers and remove the seeds and membranes. Trim the bottom slightly to help them stand upright.
3. **Parboil the Bell Peppers:**
   - Bring a large pot of salted water to a boil. Submerge the bell peppers in the boiling water for about 3-4 minutes to parboil them. This will soften the peppers slightly. Remove them and drain.
4. **Prepare the Filling:**
   - In a large skillet, heat a bit of olive oil over medium heat. Add the diced onions and cook for 2-3 minutes until they become translucent.
   - Add the ground beef and garlic to the skillet. Cook until the meat is browned and crumbled. Drain any excess fat.
   - Stir in the cooked rice, diced tomatoes (with their juices), dried oregano, dried basil, paprika, salt, and black pepper. Simmer for a few minutes until the mixture is well combined.
5. **Stuff the Bell Peppers:**
   - Carefully fill each parboiled bell pepper with the meat and rice mixture, packing it down lightly. You can drizzle some of the liquid from the skillet over the filling if desired.
6. **Top with Cheese:**
   - Sprinkle the shredded mozzarella cheese (or your preferred cheese) over the top of each stuffed bell pepper.
7. **Bake:**
   - Place the stuffed bell peppers in a baking dish. Cover the dish with aluminum foil.
   - Bake in the preheated oven for about 25-30 minutes. Then, remove the foil and continue baking for an additional 10-15 minutes, or until the peppers are tender, and the cheese is melted and bubbly.
8. **Garnish and Serve:**
   - Remove the stuffed bell peppers from the oven and let them cool for a few minutes.
   - Garnish with fresh parsley or basil if desired.

Tuna Tartare

Ingredients:

- 8 ounces (about 225g) fresh sushi-grade tuna, diced into small cubes
- 1-2 green onions, finely chopped
- 1 small cucumber, finely diced
- 1-2 tablespoons fresh cilantro or parsley, chopped
- 1 teaspoon fresh ginger, minced
- 1 small garlic clove, minced
- 1 tablespoon soy sauce
- 1 teaspoon sesame oil
- 1/2 teaspoon sriracha or chili sauce (adjust to taste)
- 1/2 teaspoon rice vinegar or fresh lime juice
- 1 teaspoon toasted sesame seeds (optional)
- Salt and black pepper, to taste
- Avocado slices (for garnish, optional)
- Wonton crisps, crackers, or baguette slices (for serving)

Instructions:

1. **Prepare the Tuna:**
   - Start by selecting high-quality, sushi-grade tuna. Make sure it's fresh and free of any off-putting odors. Dice the tuna into small, uniform cubes. Place the diced tuna in a large mixing bowl.
2. **Season the Tuna:**
   - Add the minced fresh ginger, minced garlic, soy sauce, sesame oil, sriracha or chili sauce, and rice vinegar or fresh lime juice to the bowl with the diced tuna. Gently toss to coat the tuna evenly. Allow the mixture to marinate for a few minutes.
3. **Add the Vegetables and Herbs:**
   - Add the finely chopped green onions, diced cucumber, and chopped cilantro or parsley to the tuna mixture. Gently toss everything together until well combined.
4. **Season and Garnish:**
   - Taste the tuna tartare and adjust the seasoning, adding salt and black pepper as needed. Sprinkle toasted sesame seeds over the top for extra flavor and a delightful crunch.
5. **Chill:**
   - Refrigerate the tuna tartare for about 15-30 minutes before serving. Chilling allows the flavors to meld.
6. **Serve:**
   - Arrange the tuna tartare on individual plates or a serving platter. You can use a ring mold for a neater presentation. Garnish with avocado slices if desired.
7. **Serve with Crisps:**
   - Serve the tuna tartare with wonton crisps, crackers, or slices of baguette for scooping and added texture.

Lentil Soup

Ingredients:

- 1 cup dried green or brown lentils, rinsed and drained
- 1 medium onion, finely chopped
- 2-3 cloves garlic, minced
- 1 carrot, peeled and diced
- 1 celery stalk, diced
- 1 large potato, peeled and diced
- 1 can (14 ounces) diced tomatoes
- 6 cups vegetable or chicken broth
- 1 teaspoon ground cumin
- 1/2 teaspoon ground coriander
- 1/2 teaspoon dried thyme
- 1 bay leaf
- Salt and black pepper, to taste
- 2 tablespoons olive oil
- Juice of 1 lemon (optional)
- Fresh parsley or cilantro, for garnish (optional)

Instructions:

1. **Sauté the Aromatics:**
   - In a large soup pot, heat the olive oil over medium heat. Add the chopped onion, garlic, carrot, and celery. Sauté for about 5 minutes until the vegetables become tender and the onion is translucent.
2. **Add Lentils and Spices:**
   - Stir in the rinsed and drained lentils, ground cumin, ground coriander, dried thyme, and bay leaf. Cook for another 2-3 minutes, allowing the lentils to toast slightly.
3. **Pour in Broth and Tomatoes:**
   - Add the diced tomatoes (with their juices) and pour in the vegetable or chicken broth.
4. **Add Potatoes and Season:**
   - Stir in the diced potatoes and season the soup with salt and black pepper to taste.
5. **Simmer:**
   - Bring the soup to a boil, then reduce the heat to low. Cover the pot and let it simmer for about 30-40 minutes, or until the lentils are tender and the flavors meld together.
6. **Adjust Seasoning:**
   - Taste the soup and adjust the seasoning if needed. You can add more salt, pepper, or a squeeze of fresh lemon juice for extra brightness.
7. **Serve:**
   - Remove the bay leaf and discard it. Ladle the hot lentil soup into bowls. Garnish with fresh parsley or cilantro, if desired.

Cucumber Salad

Ingredients:

- 3-4 cucumbers, thinly sliced
- 1/2 medium red onion, thinly sliced (optional)
- 1/4 cup white vinegar
- 2 tablespoons olive oil
- 1-2 teaspoons granulated sugar (adjust to taste)
- 1 teaspoon salt (adjust to taste)
- 1/2 teaspoon black pepper
- 1-2 tablespoons fresh dill, chopped (or substitute with fresh parsley)
- 1/4 cup crumbled feta cheese (optional)
- Lemon zest (optional)

Instructions:

1. **Slice the Cucumbers and Onions:**
   - Thinly slice the cucumbers. If you're using red onion, thinly slice it as well. If you prefer a milder onion flavor, you can soak the sliced onions in cold water for about 10 minutes and then drain them.
2. **Prepare the Dressing:**
   - In a small bowl, whisk together the white vinegar, olive oil, granulated sugar, salt, and black pepper until the sugar and salt are fully dissolved. Adjust the sugar and salt to your taste. You can make the dressing more or less sweet and tangy to suit your preferences.
3. **Combine Ingredients:**
   - In a large mixing bowl, combine the sliced cucumbers and onions (if using). Pour the dressing over the vegetables and toss to coat them evenly. Let the salad sit for about 10-15 minutes to marinate.
4. **Add Fresh Dill:**
   - Just before serving, sprinkle the fresh dill over the salad. You can use fresh parsley as an alternative or in addition to dill for a different flavor.
5. **Optional Garnishes:**
   - If desired, garnish the cucumber salad with crumbled feta cheese and a bit of lemon zest for extra flavor and texture.
6. **Serve:**
   - Serve the cucumber salad as a side dish or a refreshing accompaniment to grilled meats, sandwiches, or as a light and healthy snack.

Muhammara-Stuffed Mini Peppers

Ingredients:

For the Muhammara:

- 1 cup roasted red bell peppers (from a jar or freshly roasted and peeled)
- 1 cup walnuts, toasted
- 1/4 cup breadcrumbs
- 1-2 cloves garlic, minced
- 1-2 tablespoons pomegranate molasses (adjust to taste)
- 2 teaspoons ground cumin
- 1/2-1 teaspoon red pepper flakes (adjust to taste)
- 2 tablespoons olive oil
- Salt and black pepper, to taste

For the Mini Peppers:

- 15-20 mini bell peppers, various colors if available
- Olive oil, for drizzling
- Fresh parsley, for garnish (optional)

Instructions:

Prepare the Muhammara:

1. Place the roasted red bell peppers, toasted walnuts, breadcrumbs, minced garlic, pomegranate molasses, ground cumin, and red pepper flakes in a food processor.
2. Pulse the ingredients until they are well combined and form a smooth, thick paste. You may need to scrape down the sides of the food processor a few times to ensure everything is well mixed.
3. With the food processor running, drizzle in the olive oil until the Muhammara is smooth and creamy. Add more olive oil if necessary to reach your desired consistency.
4. Taste the Muhammara and adjust the seasonings, adding salt and black pepper as needed. You can also adjust the level of spice or sweetness by adding more red pepper flakes or pomegranate molasses.

Prepare the Mini Peppers:

1. Preheat your oven to 375°F (190°C).
2. Wash and dry the mini bell peppers. Cut off the tops and remove the seeds and membranes. Make sure the peppers are clean and dry inside.
3. Fill each mini pepper with the Muhammara mixture. You can use a small spoon or a pastry bag to make this process easier.
4. Place the stuffed mini peppers on a baking sheet and drizzle them with a bit of olive oil.
5. Bake in the preheated oven for about 15-20 minutes or until the peppers are tender and slightly blistered.
6. Remove the stuffed mini peppers from the oven and garnish them with fresh parsley, if desired.
7. Serve the Muhammara-stuffed mini peppers as an appetizer or snack. They can be enjoyed warm or at room temperature.

Babaganoush-Stuffed Mini Pitas

Ingredients:

For the Baba Ghanoush:

- 2 medium eggplants
- 2 cloves garlic, minced
- 2-3 tablespoons tahini
- Juice of 1 lemon
- 2 tablespoons olive oil
- 1/2 teaspoon ground cumin
- Salt and black pepper, to taste
- Fresh parsley, for garnish (optional)

For the Mini Pitas:

- Mini pita bread rounds
- Olive oil, for brushing
- Za'atar seasoning (optional)

Instructions:

Prepare the Baba Ghanoush:

1. Preheat your oven to 400°F (200°C).
2. Place the whole eggplants on a baking sheet and roast them in the oven for about 40-50 minutes or until the skin is charred, and the flesh is tender.
3. Remove the eggplants from the oven and let them cool. Once they're cool enough to handle, peel off the charred skin and discard it.
4. Place the peeled eggplants in a food processor. Add the minced garlic, tahini, lemon juice, olive oil, ground cumin, salt, and black pepper.
5. Pulse the ingredients until they form a smooth and creamy mixture. You may need to scrape down the sides of the food processor to ensure everything is well mixed.
6. Taste the baba ghanoush and adjust the seasonings if needed. Add more lemon juice, tahini, or seasonings to suit your taste.

Prepare the Mini Pitas:

1. Preheat your oven to 350°F (175°C).
2. Place the mini pita bread rounds on a baking sheet. Brush them lightly with olive oil and sprinkle with za'atar seasoning if desired for added flavor.
3. Bake the mini pitas in the preheated oven for about 5-8 minutes, or until they are warmed through and slightly crispy.

Assemble the Baba Ghanoush-Stuffed Mini Pitas:

1. Carefully cut open each mini pita to create a pocket.
2. Fill the mini pitas with a spoonful of the baba ghanoush mixture.
3. Garnish with fresh parsley, if desired, for a burst of color and freshness.
4. Serve the baba ghanoush-stuffed mini pitas as an appetizer or snack. They can be enjoyed warm or at room temperature.

Asparagus Wrapped in Prosciutto

Ingredients:

- 1 bunch of fresh asparagus spears (about 15-20 spears)
- 5-6 slices of prosciutto
- Olive oil, for drizzling
- Salt and black pepper, to taste
- Balsamic glaze, for drizzling (optional)
- Grated Parmesan cheese (optional)
- Lemon zest (optional)
- Toothpicks (for securing the prosciutto)

Instructions:

1. **Prepare the Asparagus:**
   - Wash the asparagus spears and trim the tough ends. You can do this by bending each spear; it will naturally snap at the point where the tough part ends. Discard the tough ends.
2. **Blanch the Asparagus:**
   - In a large pot, bring water to a boil. Prepare a bowl of ice water. Once the water is boiling, blanch the asparagus by placing them in the boiling water for about 1-2 minutes, just until they turn bright green. Be careful not to overcook them; they should still be crisp.
3. **Shock in Ice Water:**
   - Immediately remove the blanched asparagus from the boiling water and transfer them to the bowl of ice water to stop the cooking process. This will help the asparagus retain its vibrant green color and crispness.
4. **Wrap the Asparagus:**
   - Take 3-4 asparagus spears and bundle them together. Wrap a slice of prosciutto around the bunch to secure them. If needed, use a toothpick to hold the prosciutto in place.
5. **Drizzle with Olive Oil:**
   - Place the wrapped asparagus bundles on a baking sheet and drizzle them with a bit of olive oil. This adds a lovely flavor and helps the prosciutto crisp up when baked.
6. **Season:**
   - Season with a pinch of salt and black pepper to taste.
7. **Bake:**
   - Preheat your oven to 400°F (200°C). Bake the asparagus bundles for about 10-15 minutes or until the prosciutto becomes slightly crispy and the asparagus is tender.
8. **Optional Garnishes:**
   - If desired, drizzle the baked asparagus with balsamic glaze for a sweet tangy finish. You can also sprinkle with grated Parmesan cheese and lemon zest for added flavor.
9. **Serve:**
   - Serve the asparagus wrapped in prosciutto as an appetizer or side dish. They're best enjoyed warm.

Roasted Red Pepper Dip

Ingredients:

- 2 large red bell peppers
- 1 cup walnuts, toasted
- 1/2 cup breadcrumbs
- 2-3 cloves garlic, minced
- 2 tablespoons pomegranate molasses (substitute with lemon juice if necessary)
- 1 teaspoon ground cumin
- 1/2 teaspoon red pepper flakes (adjust to taste)
- 2-3 tablespoons olive oil
- Salt and black pepper, to taste
- Fresh parsley or mint, for garnish (optional)

Instructions:

1. **Roast the Red Bell Peppers:**
   - Preheat your oven to 450°F (230°C).
   - Place the whole red bell peppers on a baking sheet and roast them in the oven for about 20-30 minutes, turning occasionally, until the skin is charred and blistered.
2. **Steam and Peel the Peppers:**
   - Once the red bell peppers are roasted, remove them from the oven and immediately place them in a bowl. Cover the bowl with plastic wrap or a kitchen towel and let them steam for about 10-15 minutes. This makes it easier to peel the skin.
   - After steaming, peel off the charred skin, remove the seeds, and cut the peppers into small pieces.
3. **Toast the Walnuts:**
   - In a dry skillet, toast the walnuts over medium heat for a few minutes until they become fragrant. Be careful not to burn them. Let the toasted walnuts cool.
4. **Prepare the Muhammara:**
   - In a food processor, combine the roasted red bell peppers, toasted walnuts, breadcrumbs, minced garlic, pomegranate molasses (or lemon juice), ground cumin, and red pepper flakes.
5. **Pulse and Add Olive Oil:**
   - Pulse the ingredients in the food processor until they form a smooth and slightly thick mixture.
   - With the food processor running, drizzle in the olive oil to achieve your desired consistency. You can add more or less olive oil as needed.
6. **Season and Adjust:**
   - Taste the Muhammara and adjust the seasonings. Add salt and black pepper to taste. You can also adjust the level of spice, sweetness, or acidity by adding more red pepper flakes, pomegranate molasses (or lemon juice), or olive oil.
7. **Serve:**
   - Transfer the Muhammara to a serving dish and garnish with fresh parsley or mint, if desired.
8. **Enjoy:**
   - Serve your homemade roasted red pepper dip with pita bread, pita chips, or fresh vegetables for dipping.

Grilled Shishito Peppers

Ingredients:

- 8-10 ounces (about 225-280g) shishito peppers
- 1-2 tablespoons olive oil
- Salt, to taste
- Lemon wedges, for serving (optional)
- Flaky sea salt (like Maldon), for finishing (optional)

Instructions:

1. **Preheat the Grill:**
   - Preheat your grill to medium-high heat (about 400-450°F or 200-230°C). You can also use a grill pan on the stovetop if you don't have access to an outdoor grill.
2. **Prepare the Shishito Peppers:**
   - Rinse the shishito peppers and pat them dry with a paper towel. Leave the stems intact; they make for convenient handles while eating.
3. **Toss with Olive Oil:**
   - In a bowl, toss the shishito peppers with 1-2 tablespoons of olive oil until they are evenly coated. You can add a pinch of salt to the oil for extra flavor.
4. **Grill the Peppers:**
   - Place the shishito peppers directly on the grill grates or in a grill pan. Grill them for about 3-5 minutes, turning them occasionally, until they blister and become slightly charred. The cooking time may vary depending on the heat of your grill and the size of the peppers.
5. **Season and Serve:**
   - Remove the grilled shishito peppers from the grill and transfer them to a serving plate. Sprinkle with a bit of flaky sea salt if you like.
6. **Serve with Lemon Wedges:**
   - Serve the grilled shishito peppers hot, with lemon wedges on the side for squeezing over the peppers, if desired.

Printed in Great Britain
by Amazon

41698816R00057